Bear Grylls

EPIC CLIMBS

Discover more amazing books in the Bear Grylls series!

Perfect for young adventurers, the *Epic Adventures* series accompanies an exciting range of junior fiction, coloring, and activity books, and a fantastic series of *Survival Skills* handbooks to help them explore the wild. Curious kids can also learn tips and tricks for almost any extreme situation in *Survival Camp*, and explore Earth in *Extreme Planet*.

First American Edition 2019
Kane Miller, A Division of EDC Publishing

Conceived by Bonnier Books UK, in partnership with Bear Grylls Ventures
Produced by Bonnier Books UK, Suite 3.08 The Plaza, 535 King's Road, London SW10 0SZ, UK

For information contact:
Kane Miller, A Division of EDC Publishing
PO Box 470663
Tulsa, OK 74147-0663
www.kanemiller.com
www.edcpub.com
www.usbornebooksandmore.com

Library of Congress Control Number: 2019930462
Printed in Malaysia
2 4 6 8 10 9 7 5 3 1
ISBN: 978-1-61067-938-1

Disclaimer
Bonnier Books UK and Bear Grylls take pride in doing their best to get the facts right in putting together the information in this book, but occasionally something slips past their beady eyes. Therefore, we make no warranties about the accuracy or completeness of the information in the book and to the maximum extent permitted, we disclaim all liability. Wherever possible, we will endeavor to correct any errors of fact at reprint.

Kids — if you want to try any of the activities in this book, please ask your parents first! Parents — all outdoor activities carry some degree of risk and we recommend that anyone participating in these activities be aware of the risks involved and seek professional instruction and guidance. None of the health/medical information in this book is intended as a substitute for professional medical advice; always seek the advice of a qualified practitioner.

Kane Miller
A DIVISION OF EDC PUBLISHING

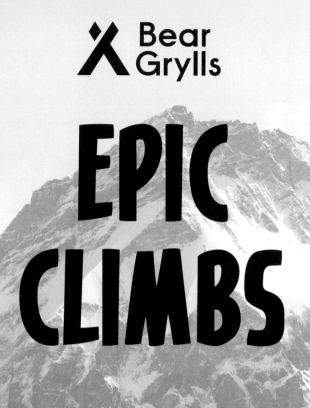

Bear Grylls

EPIC CLIMBS

CONTENTS

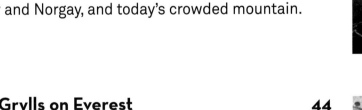

K2

Take the long trek to one of the world's most remote mountains and find out about early sightings and failed attempts, the first successful climb to the summit, and special dangers.

Denali

Before you can even begin to climb the highest mountain in North America, you will need to approach by ski along glaciers, risking dangerous crevasses, to reach the foot of the mountain.

The Matterhorn

Come face-to-face with the amazing Matterhorn, and learn about the first climb to the summit and tragedy on the descent, the ridges and faces of the mountain, the challenge of the north face, and what equipment you will need to be a successful climber.

Bear Grylls

Epic climbs

On May 26, 1996, a little after 7:00 a.m., I found myself standing somewhere that few before me had stood—at the summit of Mount Everest. This was the result of months of grueling training and hard work, and three months on the mountain itself, and I was flooded with an incomparable feeling of elation. The amazing feeling of reaching the summit of a mountain is phenomenal, and it is times like this that you are reminded of the hundreds of brave adventurers who came before you, venturing to heights nobody before them had reached, and risking their lives to conquer imposing, unforgiving peaks and stand on the very roof of the world. In this book, I explore some amazing feats by some of the most incredible climbers in history. These stories continue to inspire me to reach for my goals...

Nothing can beat the rush you get when, after hours, days, or even months, of hard work, you finally reach the summit of a mountain and look out on the landscape below. It's like being on top of the world!

It's very important to make sure you have the right gear when you're climbing any mountain. Good clothes, boots, rope, and tools can mean the difference between life and death.

Imposing peaks

Mountain climbing is an amazing experience, but it is also incredibly dangerous. Even the most experienced of climbers are at risk of injury or death from avalanches, rockfalls, and hidden crevasses, not to mention freezing temperatures and high altitudes. It is vital to train and prepare before even setting foot on a mountain, and make sure you have the right equipment with you. If you do not feel confident climbing a mountain, it might be safest to postpone your climb until you and everyone you are with are fully prepared.

The Alaska Range

NORTH AMERICA

The Rockies

The Appalachians

The Andes

SOUTH AMERICA

World mountain ranges

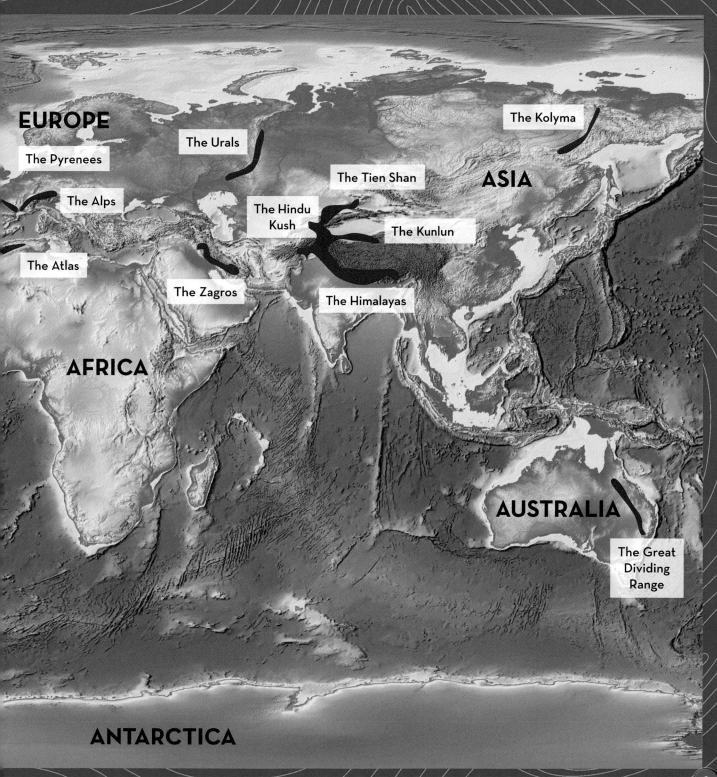

EUROPE

The Pyrenees

The Urals

The Kolyma

The Alps

The Tien Shan

ASIA

The Hindu Kush

The Kunlun

The Atlas

The Zagros

The Himalayas

AFRICA

AUSTRALIA

The Great Dividing Range

ANTARCTICA

The Eiger

The snowcapped peaks of the Bernese Alps, as seen from above.

BEAR SAYS

The north face of the Eiger is nicknamed Mordwand, meaning "murder wall," due to the high number of people who have been killed attempting to climb it.

The Ogre in the Alps

At the northern edge of the Bernese Alps sit three great peaks. Highest is the beautiful, snowy Jungfrau, also known as the Maiden, next is the Mönch (German for "the Monk"). On the left is the imposing Eiger (German for "the Ogre"), the name well describing its intimidating appearance. Unlike many other Alpine peaks, these peaks, known as the "Bernese Oberland," are easily approached, and small towns and villages dot the foothills. Because they are so easy to reach, many of these peaks were conquered by mountaineers very early—Jungfrau was first climbed as long ago as 1813. Here, nearly 50 peaks of 12,000 feet or more make a playground for alpinists and ski mountaineers.

Mont Blanc 15,771 ft.

Matterhorn 14,692 ft.

Jungfrau 13,642 ft.

Eiger 13,025 ft.

The Bernese Alps, part of the Western Alps, stretch some 70 miles east from Lake Geneva. The Eiger stands near the northeastern extremity.

The rock and ice peaks of the Bernese Oberland are a dramatic sight. Shadowed ice walls, curved faces, and sharply defined ridges loom over the valleys and plains.

Lucerne

Bern

Lake Neuchâtel

SWITZERLAND

Interlaken
▲ Eiger
13,025 ft

Lausanne

Lake Geneva

Bernese Alps

Rhone

Geneva

Matterhorn
14,692 ft.

Alps

FRANCE

Pennine

Lake
Maggiore

ITALY

Rock and ice
Among mountaineers, the Bernese Alps are known for classic ridge routes on rock and ice, and difficult north-face climbs.

Armchair climbers
Tourists can watch the climbers through telescopes from Kleine Scheidegg, a cluster of hotels and a junction of the Jungfraujoch mountain railway. This center is little more than a mile from the foot of the Eiger.

Alpine weather
Separating the largest area of glacier in the Alps from the warm European lowlands, the Oberland peaks attract fickle weather. The Eiger in particular brews its own storms. Frosty nights and clear days in summer or winter provide the safest climbing conditions, with hard snow and loose rocks solidly frozen together.

Warning clouds
This cloud sea below the Eiger is caused by a warm front meeting the cold mountains. When linked to a second layer of higher cloud, it is an early warning of bad weather.

BEAR SAYS
The southerly Föhn wind becomes warm and dry as it blows down the mountain's lee slopes, causing snow to melt and ice to become unstable. To climbers, these conditions spell danger.

Shape of the Eiger

Three main ridges and faces meet at the Eiger's summit. But its main feature is the vast, concave north face, or *Nordwand*—an intimidating maze of limestone crags and steep ice fields more than 5,900 feet high. The west flank route finds its way through rocky bands, scree terraces, and snow slopes, where loose rock is a hazard. A straightforward day climb in summer, in winter it can become an avalanche trap. The south face is a fairly difficult, slabby rock climb of 2,790 feet, while the narrow south ridge provides a good, simple route on snow and rock. The celebrated northeast ridge, the Mittellegi, gives more than a mile of strenuous, exposed rock climbing over steep towers.

A place in history

Charles Barrington, a young Irish climber, made the first ascent of the Eiger in 1858 with two expert guides, Christian Almer and Peter Bohen. They climbed the west flank, the regular route today.

Christian Almer

One of the greatest early Alpine guides, Christian Almer (1826–98) described the experience of climbing the Eiger as "unsurpassed." He made many first ascents while leading amateurs. Almer climbed all over the Alps but his favorite peak was always the Wetterhorn in his native Grindelwald Valley.

BEAR SAYS

Climbers always give names to the main features of a mountain. The steep, many armed, hanging ice field high on the Eigerwand, the focus of the north face, is known as the White Spider.

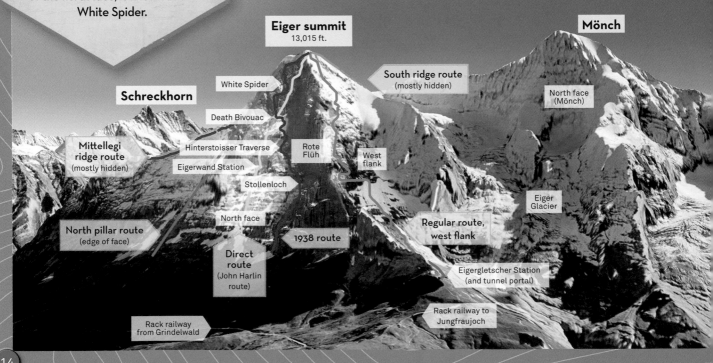

Eiger summit
13,015 ft.

Mönch

White Spider

South ridge route
(mostly hidden)

North face
(Mönch)

Schreckhorn

Death Bivouac

Mittellegi
ridge route
(mostly hidden)

Hinterstoisser Traverse

Rote
Flüh

West
flank

Eigerwand Station

Stollenloch

Eiger
Glacier

North pillar route
(edge of face)

North face

Regular route,
west flank

1938 route

Direct
route
(John Harlin
route)

Eigergletscher Station
(and tunnel portal)

Rack railway to
Jungfraujoch

Rack railway
from Grindelwald

Mittellegi Ridge

Although descended by mountaineers who ascended a different route in 1885, the narrow Mittellegi Ridge was first climbed in 1921 by Japanese alpinist Yuko Maki with three guides. Fixed ropes now ease the most difficult parts, and this climb has become a classic.

Grindelwald Valley

Nestling below spectacular mountains, the ancient village of Grindelwald is the starting point for the Jungfraujoch rack railway. It is also a major ski resort and summer vacation center, easily reached by both road and rail.

View from the window

Two trains can pass at Eismeer Station, where the picture window looks out over the magnificent glacier. Climbers bound for the Mittellegi Ridge can step out onto the ice.

Train tunnel

At Eigergletscher Station, a convenient starting place for the Eiger west-flank climb, trains leave the Alpine meadows and plunge into the dark tunnels leading into the heart of the mountain.

Trials and tragedy

By 1865, virtually all the great peaks had been climbed, and ambitious alpinists began to explore new routes on the mountains: first the ridges, then the easier-looking faces. By the 1920s, young climbers from the Alpine countries, schooled in new techniques on difficult rock, looked for fresh challenges—the great, shadowed north faces. One by one they were climbed. The Eigerwand, the Eiger's north face, long considered unclimbable, was the most intimidating objective. There was no clear line to follow up the 5,900-foot maze of extremely difficult rock and ice, raked by falling stones and often stormbound. This north face is well-known to everyone because it is so visible. For climbers on the mountain, the surrounding view takes in green foothills, wooded hillsides, a scattering of chalets in the valleys, and rich pastoral land. Only to the south is there a glimpse into the icy heart of the range.

| 1935 two dead | 1936 four dead | 1937 two safe | 1938 two dead |

Tragic first attempts

Several climbers made practice climbs to scout out the mountain, but the first serious attempt on the north face in 1935 ended when two climbers froze to death at Death Bivouac, an overhung ledge nearly halfway up the face. Four died in an epic retreat the next year, while two very experienced climbers managed a safe retreat in 1937. In 1938, a month before the first successful ascent, two Italian climbers fell and died near the "Difficult Crack."

Pathfinders
The "Traverse of the Gods" was found to be the key to the upper part of the face. It is a sequence of snowy ledges, exposed but not especially difficult, that lead to the White Spider.

Toni Kurz

Toni Kurz and Andreas Hinterstoisser teamed up with Edi Rainer and Willy Angerer to attempt the north face in 1936. Reaching a blank wall, Hinterstoisser discovered how to cross it with ropes, which the climbers removed once they were across. Angerer was injured by falling stones and they began to retreat, but were unable to recross the Hinterstoisser Traverse, so had to abseil down a 650-foot wall. On their fourth day, a storm hit. Kurz cut Willy Angerer's body free, hoping to gain more rope, but it was still too short to save him. In the storm, Hinterstoisser fell to his death and Angerer and Rainer, probably hit by stones, died of exposure, tangled in the ropes. The remaining rope was not quite long enough for Kurz to reach the rescuers below. Despite his efforts to climb down, he died there.

Portraits of the four climbers who died on the Eiger Nordwand; Edi Rainer and Willy Angerer (above), Toni Kurz and Andreas Hinterstoisser (below), 1936.

Inside the mountain

In 1897, work began on boring a tunnel four miles through the heart of the Eiger and the Mönch. It linked Kleine Scheidegg by electric railway to the ice-hung saddle of the Jungfraujoch, 4,577 feet higher. Here, an observatory was built so tourists could observe the climbers on the range. Occasional side tunnels were cut so that rubble could be tipped out. The railway, the Jungfraubahn, was completed in 1912.

There are two stations, galleries carved into the living rock, where trains pass and passengers can alight for a few minutes to admire the view from large windows set into the face of the mountain.

KEY ACHIEVEMENTS ON THE EIGER		
1938	First successful ascent	Heinrich Harrer, Fritz Kasparek, Andreas Heckmair, Ludwig Vörg
1961	First winter ascent	Toni Kinshofer, Toni Hiebeler, Anderl Mannhardt, Walter Almberger
1963	First solo ascent	Michel Darbellay
1973	First all-female rope	Wanda Rutkiewicz, Danuta Wach Stefania
2008	Fastest solo ascent	Ueli Steck

The view from the Eiger north wall, looking out over the Bernese Alps, Switzerland.

Success on the north face

Discovering a feasible, relatively safe route up the Eigerwand was a formidable problem. Max Sedlmayer and Karl Mehringer, the first to try, spent days studying the face through binoculars. The steep limestone often runs with meltwater, and the hanging ice fields are iron hard and frequently swept by falling stones. In bad weather, powder avalanches pour down the face. Safe bivouac sites are few. Hard overnight frost and settled weather are vital for a safe climb. Despite courage, and their skill on the steep limestone of the Eastern Alps, none of the Eigerwand pioneers had previously encountered climbs of this scale. Also, because the Eigerwand rises from the meadows, climbers are in the public eye—their every move can be followed by tourists and the press through telescopes at Kleine Scheidegg in the valley below.

Four at the summit

In 1938, two experienced German climbers caught up with two capable young Austrians below Death Bivouac and joined forces to make a powerful team. Despite several falls, minor injuries, a fierce storm, snow-plastered rock, and finding a route up unclimbed terrain, they reached the summit after three bivouacs. They descended safely via the west flank.

The Climbers

The successful climbers after their safe descent, left to right: Heinrich Harrer, Ludwig Vörg, Andreas Heckmair, and Fritz Kasparek. Heckmair and Vörg, both from Munich, were experienced climbers. Kasparek and Harrer, from Vienna, were younger but had fine climbing records. The four climbers were feted throughout Alpine countries and their achievement was described in *The Illustrated London News*. Many had thought the north face would never be climbed.

Rescues

Mountaineers are honor bound to assist their fellows in distress, but rescue on the Eigerwand was long considered impossible. In 1957, two Italian climbers, Claudio Corti and Stefano Longhi, were approaching the White Spider when Longhi was injured in a fall. Leaving him hanging on the rope, Corti continued to the Spider where, injured himself, he bivouacked. But the accident had been noticed, climbers mobilized from all over the Alps, and the latest rescue gear was manhandled to the summit. Alfred Hellepart was lowered 1,000 feet on a thin steel cable to piggyback Corti, after nine days on the north face, to safety. A storm broke before Longhi could be reached, and his body remained hanging there for two years.

BEAR SAYS

Rockfall is a major hazard. The cycle of freezing and thawing cracks the rock. Sun or warm weather then melts the ice, and pieces of rock fall. Avalanches of new powder snow, and other climbers above, may also dislodge stones.

Helicopters have revolutionized Alpine rescue; few places are out of reach of a rescuer swinging below a helicopter.

Amazing feat

The Corti rescue amazed the Alpine world. The Grindelwald chief guide believed that rescue was impossible, but many others disagreed. The Munich Rescue Team had the equipment, and alpinists were determined to help one of their fellows. Only a massive effort, and the courage of other climbers, saved Corti's life.

After the pioneers

Once it was known to be possible, the north-face climb was first repeated in 1947 by the great French guides Lionel Terray and Louis Lachenal, and by 13 further parties in the following decade. Tragedies still occurred, but more and more of the best alpinists succeeded on the north face, and new challenges were accepted—a winter ascent, the first solo and first female ascents, and then a direct ascent straight up the center. By the 1980s, the Eigerwand had become the goal of ambitious alpinists from every country, and the most intrepid were forging new routes. Global warming and shrinking ice fields have increased the dangers, but there are now 30 different lines. Winter has become the favorite season for climbers to try the north face. The weather is more stable, and modern clothing and equipment suit the conditions.

Champion climber
Wanda Rutkiewicz, from Poland, led the first all-female team up the Eigerwand in 1973, making the second ascent of the new North Pillar route. An experienced high-altitude mountaineer and the leading female climber of her day, she disappeared attempting a solo climb in 1992 on Kangchenjunga in the east Nepal Himalayas.

BEAR SAYS

In 1938, Alpine boots were leather and nailed, but three of the successful party also used crampons, which help to grip on the ice. Modern climbers wear insulated double boots.

List of route names

1. Lauper route
2. Scottish north-east pillar
3. Slovenian route
4. Harlin direct route
5. Metanoia
6. Japanese direct
7. 1938 route
8. Ghillini-Piola direct
9. The Swansong
10. Ochsner-Brunner route

Multiple routes

As climbers looked for fresh challenges, more new routes on the north face were tried for the first time. Each route involves many difficult sections, and reaching the summit is an achievement for even the most experienced climber.

Filming *The Eiger Sanction*

In 1974, the actor and director Clint Eastwood made the bold decision to film the novel *The Eiger Sanction*, a spy thriller set on and around the Eiger's north face. A strong team of British and American climbers and mountain cameramen joined the actors at Kleine Scheidegg and spent six weeks shooting some spectacular scenes, although the most dangerous areas of the north face were avoided.

Everest

HIMALAYA FACT FILE	
Area	380,292 square miles
Length	1,491 miles
Country borders crossed	India, Pakistan, China, Bhutan, Nepal
Major rivers that rise here	Indus, Ganges, Tsangpo/Brahmaputra, Rong, Yamuna, Chenab, Sutlej
No. of world's highest peaks	10 of the world's 14 highest

Everest

BEAR SAYS

The challenge of reaching the world's highest peak inspires hundreds of climbers annually. They plan and train for years to achieve the goal of standing on the summit of Mount Everest.

Lhotse

Nuptse

Baruntse

Imja Tse

Roof of the world

The highest mountain in the world, at a peak of 29,029 feet, Mount Everest rises out of the Himalayan mountain range, bordering China and Nepal. It was formed around 60 million years ago, when the movement of the Earth caused the ground under the sea to be pushed up, out of the water, to form towering mountains. Climbers continue to be fascinated by Everest, and use their strength and skill to scale its terrifying heights. Everest is 978 feet higher than K2, the world's second-highest mountain.

How Everest formed

The Himalayas are the youngest and highest mountain range on the planet. The theory of plate tectonics shows how the range was created from the collision of India and Asia. These plates, which slide around on the fluid-like asthenosphere, are still moving approximately 2–4 inches each year.

India starts its journey
India broke away from the great southern continent, Gondwana, about 145 million years ago and began its northward journey toward Eurasia.

Ocean-to-continent subduction
As India approached Eurasia, its seafloor began to move. A line of volcanoes developed along the edge of the Eurasian plate.

Collision begins
India was pushed against Eurasia. Seafloor rocks trapped between the continents were squashed together and pushed upward, creating the Himalayas.

Folding and uplift
The ocean floor turned to rock, and was squeezed upward and outward. This continues today.

What is Everest made of?

Unbelievably, the summit of Mount Everest is actually made up of marine limestone, part of an ancient seabed that now sits on top of huge rocks. The top of the world's highest mountain is, in fact, covered with the fossils of deep-sea life. When climbers plant their flags on the snowy summit, that snow lies over rock containing the skeletal remains of creatures that fell to the seabed, fossilized 200 million years ago, and were then thrust upward by the collision of continental plates. Sir Edmund Hillary verified that the rocks within the top 3,280 feet of Mount Everest contain fossilized seashells.

Fossil proof
Until recently, the theory of plate tectonics was just that—a theory. No one could prove it until explorers, such as those who attempted Mount Everest, were able to bring back rock samples from the summit for geologists to study. Their theory was proven by the fossil evidence.

Peaks and rivers

Everest
Close to the summit of Mount Everest, the rock is made of marine limestone.

Rongbuk Glacier
The Rongbuk Glacier system is the main way to the northern foot of the mountain. Climbers follow the East Rongbuk Glacier on their way to the North Col and the north ridge.

Nuptse
Also known as West Peak, Nuptse sits opposite the great flank of Everest. Camps 1 and 2 are dwarfed by its fearsome precipices.

Rong River
The Rong drains the entire Rongbuk Glacier system northward. But, instead of joining the mighty Tsangpo River, which flows alongside the Himalayas to the north, it flows into the Arun, one of several rivers which, having cut gorges through the Himalayan range, flow eventually to the Ganges.

George Leigh Mallory

Conquering Everest

Of the climbers who have tried—and failed—to reach Everest's peak, two of the most famous are George Leigh Mallory and Andrew Irvine. Mallory was the shining star of British climbing, and was attempting this climb with 22-year-old Andrew Irvine. On June 8, 1924, a few days before Mallory's 38th birthday, and tantalizingly close to the summit of Everest, Mallory and Irvine disappeared without a trace. Mallory's body wasn't found until 75 years later, and there has been no trace of Irvine's body, nor of the camera they had with them, since. Some people still believe they might have reached the summit and died on the way down, but nobody knows exactly what happened up on the mountain.

TIMELINE OF EVENTS IN THE 1920S		
1921	**1922**	**1924**
A team of British climbers climbed part of Everest's north face and saw the sweeping East Rongbuk Glacier. They climbed by this route and reached the North Col.	The British made another attempt on Everest. Mallory led one team without extra oxygen and reached 26,903 feet. A second team, on a slightly different line, reached 27,297 feet using extra oxygen.	At the third British attempt, George Mallory and Andrew Irvine climbed higher than all previous British attempts, but disappeared. Two other team members, Howard Somervell and Edward Norton, also made an attempt. Norton, alone, reached 28,117 feet, without extra oxygen, before turning back.

Seventy-five years after the disappearance of Mallory and Irvine, an American team set out to search for their bodies. Years before, in 1933, Irvine's ice ax had been found below the First Step. In 1975, a Chinese climber said he had seen a body, probably that of an Englishman, and which seemed to have been there for a long time, high on the mountain. The American team took these clues into account and planned the search carefully. Within the first two days, they found Mallory's body. His clothing still carried his name tag. His distinctive nailed boots from the 1920s were still largely intact.

Mallory's climbing boots, nailed with clinkers for rock climbing.

Discovered at a height of 26,772 feet, the body of Mallory showed signs of injury. He had a deep wound on his forehead, a broken leg, and bruising around his waist from the climbing rope he had used.

First to the top

In March 1953, 350 Nepalese porters brought supplies to a camp at Thyangboche Monastery, Nepal, below Mount Everest. The camp at Thyangboche was the appointed meeting place for the new British team who were to attempt the summit. Twenty years earlier, in April 1933, two British biplanes with supercharged engines had attempted to fly over Everest's peak, but had almost been destroyed on the mountain by the violent, hurricane-force winds near the summit. Everest was continuing to repel all would-be summiteers, either airborne or on foot.

Preparing to climb

The 1953 British Expedition team assembled at the British Embassy in Kathmandu in the first week of March. From the Indian railhead, the team brought their 473 expedition packages on Indian trucks, in stifling heat, to the Nepalese border. Here, they loaded every package onto the overhead ropeway, and winched it into the valley of Kathmandu. Among the packages was a large bundle containing double-layer goose-down sleeping bags from New Zealand, which Edmund Hillary had arranged for members of the expedition to use. These sleeping bags proved themselves worth their weight in gold when it came to surviving a night in subzero temperatures on Mount Everest.

Edmund Hillary
At age 16, Edmund had his first experience of mountains and snow on a school ski trip in his homeland, New Zealand. Now, aged 33, he was hoping for a chance to scale the highest mountain on the planet.

Tenzing Norgay
In 1952, Tenzing, with Swiss climber Raymond Lambert, had succeeded in climbing higher than any other climber to attempt Everest—but the peak had still eluded him.

Each person on the 1953 British Expedition team had a specific set of responsibilities. Without such strong teamwork, it is unlikely that Hillary and Norgay would have succeeded. Behind the two men who made the summit was a team of committed, skilled mountaineers.

Bid for the summit

With the final challenge facing them, Hillary and Norgay watched their support team head back down to Advanced Base Camp 4. After years of preparation and teamwork, it was now up to the two of them to make history. In the end, they were only on the summit for around 15 minutes, but those precious, hard-won moments changed both their lives forever.

Well-earned victory
At 11:30 a.m., on May 29, 1953, the two men reached the summit at last, and Hillary took this iconic picture of his climbing partner on the roof of the world.

National heroes
After their success, Hillary and Norgay returned to the UK as heroes.

Into the death zone

Even without the perilous weather, Everest is full of dangers. Some climbers fall, some are frozen to death, some suffer from altitude sickness and need emergency aid to get them off the mountain to recover. Everest is in the so-called "death zone" because the oxygen there is so thin that the body starts dying through lack of it. Getting to the summit and back down quickly, to more oxygenated air, is the only way to survive.

North Col route

The north ridge from North Col is the route that Mallory and Irvine took in 1924, and was successfully climbed again in 1960 by a Chinese party. The famous Chinese ladder is in permanent position at the Second Step—a vertical 26-foot wall—which is a constant cause of traffic jams of climbers. The north ridge and the north face rise above the East Rongbuk Glacier, which has to be climbed en route to the summit.

The Himalayas
The biggest terrestrial mountain range on the planet, containing 10 of the 14 highest mountains in the world, as viewed from above.

The roof of the world

At the summit of the highest mountain, in the world's highest mountain range, climbers stand on marine limestone—rock that was once on the seafloor. As the Eurasian and Indo-Australian plates collided 60 million years ago, the seafloor was pushed upward. The pressure continues to push the mountains higher to this day.

Climate in the Himalayas

Hundreds of peaks rise higher than 23,000 feet in the Himalayas, many still unclimbed and even unnamed. Bringing the rains to the Indian subcontinent, the summer monsoon falls as heavy snow on the higher mountains, while the northern flanks, in the rain shadow, are not much affected. Summer and winter snows feed the glaciers that give birth to many of Asia's great rivers.

South Col route

Since the summit of Everest was first reached in 1953, hundreds of climbers have followed this route to the top. Some say that the South Col route is a little more dangerous than the north ridge route, mainly because the Khumbu Icefall is so unstable. The route through the icefall changes daily, as it is constantly moving. In the dawn, the safest time, the cold in the icefall and the Western Cwm is intense, but by midday the sun reflecting from the snowy flanks of Everest, Lhotse, and Nuptse can raise the air temperature to as much as 100°F. The climb up the Lhotse face requires a major effort, and tired climbers clip on to fixed ropes to assist the ascent and safeguard against falls. Climbers usually start using oxygen above Camp III, before the route bears upward and across to the South Col.

BEAR SAYS

The teamwork between Tenzing and Hillary was essential to their successful climb; both were true team players. It was the teamwork shown by the entire expedition that really made the successful climb possible.

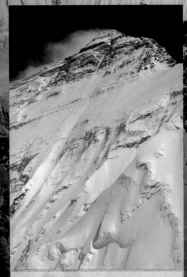

North face of Mount Everest, Chomolungma, from 19,685 feet, Lho La, Rongbuk Glacier, Tibet.

Key

⬤ Summit

▬ South Col route

▬ North ridge route

△3 Camp number

②　 Points of interest

Lhotse
27,940 ft.

Lhotse face ①

South Col ⑥ ④ ③ Nuptse

Everest summit
29,029 ft.

Hillary Step ⑤

Second Step ②

Kangshung face

Western Cwm ④

West ridge

Advanced Base Camp ②

North

Northeast ridge ⑤

North ①

North ridge ④

Khumbu Icefall ⑦

North Col ③ ③

South Col route

South Base Camp ⑧

Advanced Base Camp ②

East Rongbuk Glacier ⑨

North ridge route

①

Rongbuk Glacier

⑫

Khumbu Glacier

Rongbuk monastery

⑩

North Base Camp ⑪

Lhotse face

The 4,265-foot Lhotse face rears up at the head of the Western Cwm. The route up it, although not especially steep, is unrelenting ice, broken only by a few crevasses. It is usual to establish Camp III at half height and to fix ropes over most of the route.

Second Step

The north ridge merges with the northeast ridge where climbers face the Second Step at 28,199 feet. It is a desperately difficult 26-foot rock wall. Many people wonder if Mallory managed to climb it. Today, most climbers use the metal ladder left by the Chinese.

North Col

Steep snow slopes lead 886 feet up to the North Col, the snowy saddle at 23,196 feet separating the north ridge from the peak of Changtse. A bleak, windswept place, it is nevertheless a good location for a camp at the start of the main climb.

Western Cwm

Two miles long, walled by the icy faces of Everest, Lhotse, and Nuptse, the Western Cwm is a gently sloping glacial valley, the highest in the world. Often stiflingly hot by day, always bitterly cold at night, Camp 2 is placed here, usually at around 21,000 feet.

Hillary Step

The Hillary Step was a 66-foot rock buttress blocking the narrow ridge just below the summit. Hillary climbed the steep and very exposed chimney that split it, but in later years climbers were assisted by fixed ropes. Sadly, this piece of mountaineering history was probably destroyed in the devastating earthquake that hit Nepal in 2015.

South Col

Camp 4 on the bare, wind-blasted South Col, the 25,938-foot saddle between Everest and Lhotse, is the key to the ascent. From here, climbers attempt the summit. But it is no place to stay longer than absolutely necessary.

Khumbu Icefall

This icefall is a labyrinth of massive ice towers, cracking and collapsing as the glacier tumbles 1,969 feet down to the almost flat Khumbu Glacier below. An experienced climber takes six or seven hours to climb through it.

South Base Camp

At 17,552 feet, among the Khumbu Glacier moraines below the icefall, Southern Base Camp is no place for a holiday. The altitude makes proper rest difficult, but yak trains bring up appetizing food and there are even hot showers to make conditions comfortable.

East Rongbuk Glacier

Rubble covered, then covered with ice pinnacles, the East Rongbuk Glacier leads to Advanced Base Camp at the foot of the North Col. Exploring here in 1921, Mallory thought the North Col might be the key to the summit.

Rongbuk monastery

The monastery lies at the foot of the Rongbuk Glacier. It is the highest monastery in the world, and is passed by all climbers who climb Everest by the north ridge route. About 60 Buddhist monks and nuns live here, meditating among the most dramatic scenery in the world.

North Base Camp

Base Camp for the north ridge route lies below the snout of the Rongbuk Glacier. The route itself is straightforward, and a ladder helps with the only serious difficulty, the Second Step. But nothing at high altitude is ever "easy"—even one step upward may demand several breaths.

Rongbuk Glacier

Climbers must first trek up the moraines beside the Rongbuk Glacier before branching off up the tributary East Rongbuk Glacier. Most glaciers like this have been shrinking during the past century, due to global warming.

BEAR SAYS

Yaks are strong, and very sure-footed on mountains. They are used to carry heavy loads of gear to the base camps.

To the summit without oxygen

Reinhold Messner had already reached the summit of many of the world's highest mountains when he decided to do something no one had done before—climb to the summit of Mount Everest alone, and without the help of extra oxygen. Most climbers use oxygen, carried in cylinders in their backpacks, to help them cope with the thin air above 23,000 feet. Only by conditioning his body so that it became used to functioning at high altitudes could Messner possibly hope to achieve his goal. The plan to climb alone was also a major challenge. There would be no support in case of difficulty or danger, not even someone to help put up the tent for an overnight camp.

An Italian from the German-speaking South Tyrol, Messner was the first man to climb all fourteen 26,250-foot peaks. He is considered one of the most accomplished mountaineers of all time.

MESSNER'S ASCENTS OF THE WORLD'S HIGHEST PEAKS		
1970	Nanga Parbat, Pakistan	26,657 ft.
1972	Manaslu, Nepal	26,781 ft.
1975	Gasherbrum, Pakistan/China	26,470 ft.
1977	Dhaulagiri*, Nepal	26,795 ft.
1978	Mount Everest, Nepal/China	29,035 ft.
1979	K2, Pakistan/China	28,251 ft.
1980	Mount Everest**, Nepal/China	29,035 ft.
1981	Shisha Pangma, China	26,398 ft.
1982	Kanchenjunga, Nepal/India	28,169 ft.
1982	Gasherbrum II, Pakistan/China	26,362 ft.
1982	Broad Peak, Pakistan/China	26,401 ft.
1983	Cho Oyu, Nepal/China	26,906 ft.
1985	Annapurna, Nepal	26,545 ft.
1985	Dhaulagiri, Nepal	26,795 ft.
1986	Makalu, Nepal/China	27,766 ft.
1986	Lhotse, Nepal/China	27,940 ft.

All without extra oxygen. *Summit not reached ** Solo

The "death zone" near the summit is so-called because the body quite literally starts to die through lack of oxygen. Tenzing Norgay and Hillary are pictured here with oxygen cylinders and masks.

BEAR SAYS

When skin is exposed to temperatures below 32°F, there is danger of frostbite. The fingers, toes, nose, and ears are particularly susceptible.

What is thin air?

The air we breathe contains 21 percent oxygen, which humans, animals, and plants all need. At sea level, we can breathe comfortably because the air pressure allows us to take in as much air as we need without effort. But at higher altitudes, such as on mountains of more than 8,200 feet, the air pressure decreases and the air becomes thinner. Each breath a person takes at those heights contains less oxygen than a breath taken at sea level. It is difficult to breathe in enough air to receive the oxygen needed for normal activity, and the effort itself is exhausting.

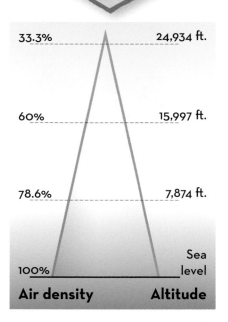

33.3%	24,934 ft.
60%	15,997 ft.
78.6%	7,874 ft.
100%	Sea level

Air density   **Altitude**

Reinhold Messner points to a photograph of Mount Everest after his unprecedented solo ascent without supplementary oxygen, 1980.

Acclimatization

One of the keys to climbing, and surviving, at high altitudes is to allow the body to become acclimatized to thin air. For this reason, many climbers spend a couple of weeks at higher-than-usual altitudes before tackling a high-altitude climb. Gradually, their blood adapts to the conditions and is able to carry more oxygen than usual in each red blood cell. Practice climbs are helpful in other ways as well; a climber can carry equipment up to a high camp for use during the final ascent. Reinhold Messner spent seven weeks at an altitude of more than 16,400 feet, becoming acclimatized to the thin air before his solo ascent in 1980. Two years earlier, he had made the first oxygen-free ascent, with climbing partner Peter Habeler.

At more than 16,400 feet, dozens of tents from several different expeditions are crowded together on the flattest places that can be found amid the piles of unstable rubble of huge glacial moraines. Base Camp teams keep up the morale of climbers by providing good food, comfortable tents, and even hot showers.

Crowded mountain

The first ascent of a mountain, or of a new route on it, is the most challenging one. Every subsequent climber knows that it can be climbed. Until 1970, only 28 climbers had reached the summit of Everest on just six successful expeditions. Twenty years later, a dozen different routes had been pioneered, some of them quite difficult. During the 1980s, there were many more attempts. The two original routes were straightforward, although serious, climbs, and soon commercial expeditions were offering guided ascents. By 2000, more than

When climbing conditions are good, many climbing teams reach the summit on one day, sometimes approaching from different sides of the mountain. This causes a "traffic jam" both on the climbing routes and at the summit.

1,100 climbers had reached the summit, sometimes dozens on the same day if the weather was good. That pattern continues today, and the number of people climbing Everest during the most suitable weather is increasing.

With guided expeditions leading climbers to the summit, dozens of climbers may be on the mountain on the same day. This causes delays on the fixed-ropes sections where progress must be one at a time.

What triggers an avalanche?

An avalanche can happen wherever snow is lying at a steep angle, on slopes of 30–45°, but large avalanches can also occur on slopes as gentle as 25°. Snow is unstable during and after snowfalls, or after prolonged heating by the sun, especially on steep inclines, and snow falling at a rate of one inch or more per hour increases the risk of avalanche. Most frightening are ice avalanches, which are unpredictable. Himalayan ice cliffs are "rubbery," tending to lean a long way before they finally collapse, hurling down huge chunks of ice that sweep all before them.

Mountain weather

Everest rises into the jet stream, the narrow band of very high winds that frequently encircles the planet at that latitude above 26,247 feet, so any attempt on the summit is governed by both wind and weather. Apart from the usual winter snowfall, the Nepal Himalayas are also subject to the summer monsoon, which brings a second season of heavy snowfall to the mountains from June until early September. Originally it was thought that there was only one weather window for climbing, in the short period of calm before the onset of the monsoon in early June. But, in the 1950s, it was realized that there is another fairly stable period after the monsoon in late September. In fact, post-monsoon weather is typically more stable, though far colder, than pre-monsoon weather. Modern clothing and equipment help climbers to withstand the cold, and there are now two official weather windows on Everest: pre- and post-monsoon.

WEATHER CONDITIONS ON EVEREST	
Temperature	January: Summit temperature averages −32°F; it can be as low as −76°F
	July: Summit temperature averages −2°F
Wind speed	October–March: Almost constant Category 1 hurricane (93 mph)
	June–September: Almost no wind at all (15 mph)

J F M A M J J A S O N D
X⊕ -32°F   X⊕ -29°F

This mountain is best climbed in May and June or September

The extreme altitude means that the air temperature is much lower than in most other places on Earth.

Bear Grylls

Climbing Mount Everest

I first saw the majestic Himalayan mountain range while hiking with a friend in northern India. It stood in the distance, a white pinnacle against a deep-blue sky. It was such an alluring sight, a beckoning finger tempting me toward the roof of the world with the promise of ultimate adventure. While parachuting in southern Africa, my chute failed to open fully and I hit the ground hard, fracturing three vertebrae. At the age of 23, there was a chance I would never walk properly again. But, digging deep within myself, I finally got back on my feet, motivated by that vivid image of Mount Everest, which was immortalized on a poster on my wall at home. It represented a chance to prove myself physically and heal myself emotionally. I would be following in the footsteps of some legendary adventurers in years gone by. It was going to be a life-changing adventure.

There are few experiences as mind-blowing as finally standing at the peak of a mountain, looking out on the world below.

Known as "the roof of the world," Everest is the highest peak on the planet. Remarkably, this was once a prehistoric seabed.

The Himalayan Range
Ten of the 14 tallest mountains in the world are located in the Himalayas.

Everest is part of the Himalayan Range, which stretches 15,000 miles from Pakistan to Tibet, boasting most of the world's tallest peaks. Everest itself sits on the Mahālangūr Himāl section. The range is so massive that it even controls the weather to the south. Due to tectonic plate movement, it is growing at a rate of 0.2 inches every year.

Roof of the world

Known as Sagarmatha by the Nepalese, Chomolungma by the Chinese, and Peak XV in the West, before being named Everest in 1865, this formidable peak stands at 29,029 feet, and is the tallest point on Earth. It beats the second-highest mountain, K2, by over 750 feet.

Everest
29,029 ft.

K2
28,251 ft.

Extreme weather
Summit winds have been recorded at 174 mph. Temperatures range from 3.2°F to -41°F. The air is thin, with only 33 percent of the oxygen available at sea level.

Victims and failures

As of 2016, there have been 286 deaths recorded on Everest. Climbers from across the globe have lost their lives chasing their dreams. The weather can change in moments: blizzards, hurricane-force winds, plunging temperatures, and electrical storms. Combine this with avalanches, deep crevasses, sheer ice faces, and lack of oxygen, and the chances of summit success are low.

Eternal rest

Many bodies remain on the flanks of Everest, as it's too difficult to bring them down. The thin air and freezing temperatures preserve them in their final resting states. Many memorials can be found at Base Camp for those lost on the mountain.

BEAR SAYS

George Mallory was famously asked why he wanted to climb Everest. He replied, "Because it's there!" Only when you see Everest for yourself can you understand its allure.

George Mallory

Experienced climber George Mallory led the first three British expeditions to Everest. He vanished, along with 22-year-old Andrew Irvine, in 1924, close to the summit. It is unknown if they ever made it or not. Mallory's body was not discovered until 1999, and Irvine's was never found.

The route

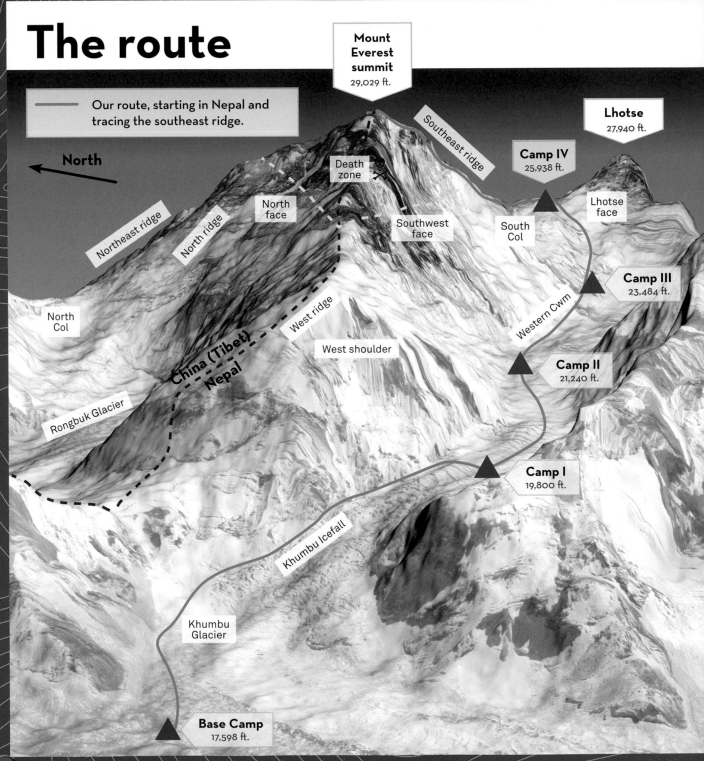

Mount Everest summit
29,029 ft.

Lhotse
27,940 ft.

Our route, starting in Nepal and tracing the southeast ridge.

← **North**

Southeast ridge

Camp IV
25,938 ft.

Northeast ridge

North ridge

North face

Death zone

Southwest face

South Col

Lhotse face

Camp III
23,484 ft.

North Col

West ridge

China (Tibet)
Nepal

West shoulder

Western Cwm

Camp II
21,240 ft.

Rongbuk Glacier

Camp I
19,800 ft.

Khumbu Icefall

Khumbu Glacier

Base Camp
17,598 ft.

South Summit

At 28,704 feet, the South Summit is the second-highest peak in the world—higher than the second-highest mountain, K2.

Lhotse

At 27,940 feet, Lhotse is the fourth-highest peak in the world, and is connected to Everest by the South Col.

BEAR SAYS

After my parachute accident, I was determined not only to get back on my feet, but to summit Everest as proof to myself that every challenge can be overcome.

Sir Edmund Hillary had once described the mountain of Ama Dablam as "unclimbable"... so I was determined to climb it.

Preparation

Getting ready for this mission wasn't just a simple task of gathering the right gear and starting to climb. Your body needs to get used to the altitude over time through steady acclimatization. Routes were carefully planned, and with this came the realization that this is not a straightforward journey up. Because of the altitude, we would be pushing up high, then sleeping at high altitude to experience the effects of the thin air, and then climbing back down the next morning to give our bodies a chance to recover. Our ascent would be a series of dangerous maneuvers up and down the mountain, until we reached the summit.

Ama Dablam

Located in East Nepal, Ama Dablam was my first taste of altitude. At a mere 22,349 feet, it was a baby compared to Everest. The thin air causes constant migraines, which fog concentration. No matter how fit I thought I was, I was exhausted by the time I reached the summit. It had taken a lot out of me. And up there, I saw the distant peak of Everest towering 6,680 feet above where I was now. It was very daunting!

Equipment

Climbing is technical, not just physical, and the array of equipment that climbers must carry can be extensive. Aside from thermal gear, you need food, a stove to cook it on, tents, crampons (that attach to your boots, allowing you to grip onto the ice), carabiners, hammers, ice screws, ropes, goggles, a roll mat, a sleeping bag, a headlamp (and spare batteries), and then, on top of all that, you have heavy oxygen tanks.

BEAR SAYS

As I learned from my disastrous parachute jump, the only person you can really rely on to look after your equipment is yourself. Check and check again.

Sherpas

The wonderful Sherpa people are the not-so-secret weapon in every attempt to scale Everest. They have adapted to living at high altitude, and are undoubtedly the greatest mountaineers in the world. Living at such extreme heights means they are incredibly fit and have a greater ability to function on limited amounts of oxygen.

The Sherpa people

Many Sherpa people have only one name. Due to a mix-up in Nepal's census, many were accidentally assigned the surname "Sherpa."

Base Camp

Arriving at Base Camp was like arriving at a large, tented village. The thin air was filled with nervous excitement, as climbers assembled for the most daunting moment of their lives. We were in the company of more than 40 climbers from around the globe—Singapore, Mexico, Russia, and Bolivia to name but a few— men and women ready, as I was, to risk everything to reach the top.

A splash of color on top of the world
Base Camp's mass of multicolored tents and Buddhist prayer flags is a welcome sight from the stark white peaks.

Psyching up

Days spent at Base Camp were used to discuss strategy and talk to other climbers who had already made the ascent. With each day I woke to watch the clouds part from the iconic peak, and I was so anxious to get underway.

First steps

On April 7, I finally set off to chase my dream. I was climbing with a Sherpa named Nima, and my childhood friend Mick Crosthwaite. We moved with purpose, determined looks fixed to our faces ... yet we had no idea what the mountain had in store for us.

Facing some of the harshest conditions on Earth, it was hard not to be nervous as I set off.

Khumbu Icefall

Crampons on, we clambered through the Khumbu Icefall. House-sized chunks of ice stretched up and away into the distance, and the groan of the shuffling glacier reverberated through the still air. As the gradient increased, we roped ourselves together. Looking back down, we could see that Base Camp was already a speck on the ice. Now the adrenaline was really flowing.

A river of ice

The trick to crossing the Khumbu Icefall is to attempt it before sunrise, as it is colder and more stable during the night, and is therefore less likely to move.

Crevasses

Massive crevasses open up in the constantly shifting ice. They plunge into pitch darkness and are almost impossible to escape from. The Sherpas have placed a network of temporary aluminum ladders over the drops, fixed in place with ropes and ice screws. The only way to cross these is by placing one foot in front of the other... and not looking down. Confidence is key.

Camp I

Ahead lay Camp I. The only problem was that the ladders crossing the final crevasse hung limply, having been torn apart by the shifting ice. Light was fading, and it was too late to find a new way across. Mick and I decided to turn around and head back to Base Camp. After nine hours of climbing, we were battered and needed time to recover.

Ice ladders

No matter how many times you cross these ladders, your heart is in your mouth.

BEAR SAYS

Respect is the key word up here. Respect the mountain and respect the weather. If you have doubts about safety, head back down, and live another day.

The drop

Suddenly, I felt the ground tremble. With a whispering sound, a crack in the ice opened between my legs, and I plummeted into a hidden crevasse. I was briefly knocked unconscious, and woke to find myself dangling from my rope. Luckily, Nima and Mick were able to haul me back up. Returning to Base Camp, my confidence was shattered, and a piece of bone had chipped from my elbow in the fall. I had barely started, and already Everest was chewing me up.

Valley of silence

The brush with death had knocked my confidence, but I was determined not to give up. Starting again from Base Camp, we pressed on, back up into the Khumbu Icefall. It wasn't any easier, and this time we carried more supplies, as we had no intention of returning to camp.

Breathless

Altitude was already playing its tricks. Constant headaches made focusing on even the simplest tasks difficult, and the higher we got, the shorter our breaths became. The air is so dry that it sucks moisture from your mouth, and pretty soon everybody had an irritating dry cough that simply wouldn't go away. We powered on to Camp I, and then to Camp II.

Western Cwm
"Cwm," pronounced "coom," is the Welsh word for "valley."

Camp II

After a strenuous seven-hour push, we reached Camp II, exhausted. Sleep was fleeting—the mind was willing, but the body was constantly twitching, crying out for more oxygen. While shivering the next morning, I was rewarded with a glorious sight that reminded me why I was putting myself through all this punishment. The first rays of dawn tickled Everest's peak, now visible ahead of us. I felt like I could almost reach out and touch it.

BEAR SAYS

Frostbite is a danger in the cold. The skin is literally frozen and the damage is irreversible. Ensuring proper protection is the only way of avoiding this.

At these heights you sleep fully clothed, only taking off your outer boots. Your inner boots stay firmly on, or frostbite can get to you.

The silence

The valley is covered with scree rocks and ice, which constantly shifts underfoot. For every three steps we took, we'd slide back two. Fortunately, the rocks soon turned back to ice, and we were able to make steadier progress. It is understandable why they call it the Valley of Silence. The raised slopes protect you from the harsh winds and absorb every sound. It's both eerie and bewitching.

Camp III

We finally reached Camp III and crawled inside the tents our Sherpas had helped set up two days earlier. Now out of the Western Cwm, the wind blew hard and brought heavy snow. We drifted in and out of a fitful sleep, huddled together in a tent that was far too small for three.

A wall of blue ice
When snow on a glacier is compressed, the air bubbles that make ice appear white are squeezed out. The ice then appears blue in color.

The Lhotse face

Above us now lay the formidable Lhotse face: a 16,145-foot sheer blue ice wall. This is a demanding and grueling technical climb—five hours of calf-straining, lung-burning, arm-wrenching exercise. The view was dizzying, but once again it was also a reminder never to look down.

Back to Earth

The next morning brought a perfect stillness and an epic view. The Himalayan Range stretched before us, their peaks either level with or below us. Other than Everest, there was nothing higher on the planet. So it was with aching bodies we descended again—this was our final acclimatization step before we tried for the very summit itself.

Storm warning

Back at Base Camp, we prepared for our final ascent. This would be a make-or-break push to the summit. At this stage, more than any other, we were reliant on a break in the weather. Clouds covering the peak meant we didn't stand a chance at achieving our goal. The winds would be far too strong to be able to climb at all. We waited impatiently for the detailed weather reports ...

The weather window

For just a few days in May, the wind speeds reduce and the snows ease up. This gives narrow opportunity for climbers to reach the summit.

BEAR SAYS

If you are unlucky enough to be caught in an avalanche, try to cup your hand over your mouth to create an air pocket so you don't suffocate.

Avalanches

Avalanches are one of the biggest killers on any mountain. They have many causes—too much snow, a crevasse opening, furious winds displacing ice—but the results are often fatal.

The push for glory

While waiting back at Base Camp, I fell ill with a chronic chest infection and had to take antibiotics. News came that the wind was beginning to ease and the clouds were clearing away. We had five days to make Camp IV so we'd be in position when the weather finally broke. But still vomiting and drained, I couldn't go. The rest of the team set off. Feeling so distraught not to be with them, I shook their hands as they set off, leaving me behind.

Typhoon warning

Two days later, I knew my friends would now be heading to Camp III. That's when a weather warning came in: a typhoon was approaching. In a couple of days, it would reach us and potentially strand the party. With nobody up there to help, they would be in real danger. I had recovered enough by now, so I headed up to be in a position to help if things turned bad, and to be ready to shoot for the summit if the weather held off long enough.

Crisis at altitude

While at Camp II, I received a call from Mick—the team had run out of oxygen, just 295 feet from the top. The winds were now too strong to continue up. I was helpless as I listened to them say they only had 10 minutes to live unless they found more oxygen. Mick then slipped and fell, tumbling for over 500 feet down the ice and snow face. By a miracle, he stopped on a small patch of deep snow and was rescued by two Swedish climbers and a Sherpa carrying spare oxygen. I was so relieved to hear that Mick and my buddy Neil Laughton were heading down, exhausted but alive.

BEAR SAYS

You burn 10,000–20,000 calories every day while climbing, so the fattiest foods are good for you up here!

Cooking on Everest

Cooking warm food isn't easy at the top of the world. The Sherpas use these clever solar cookers to make hot food. It's important to stay warm and keep your spirits up.

Reaching the summit

then spent many days waiting alone in my tent at Camp II, hoping that the weather might ease up again for me to be able to make an attempt on the summit. A typhoon was headed our way. A few days later, we received the news we were waiting for. The typhoon had changed course—we had our shot at the top! I knew in my bones I could do this. I just hoped the mountain would allow me up.

One large step for a man ...
The Hillary Step—the last obstacle to victory.

Endurance

With oxygen masks on, we climbed into higher and higher terrain. We were now in what is called the death zone, where our bodies literally began to die. Sucking in the thin air burned my lungs, and with the masks trickling a feeble 70 ounces of air per minute, I was gasping for breath. Pushing up and over the Yellow Band, a sandstone rock that once used to be a seabed, we were now moving so slowly. They call it the "Everest Shuffle": two paces up, rest, two paces up, rest.

Standing on the roof of the world

Leaving our final high camp, Camp IV at 26,247 feet, it was pitch dark. We climbed all through the night. Up and up. The final 393-foot ridge was like walking on a knife blade—Tibet on one side, Nepal on the other. I made the mistake of looking down. My heart was in my mouth, I was so scared. Every step was punishing. But I kept going. Then, finally, at 7:22 a.m. on May 26, 1996, I reached the summit. The achievement had physically pushed me beyond my limits, but I had climbed Everest, and healed myself.

Back to earth

Pausing for a quick photograph and a moment to appreciate a vista so immense that you can see the curvature of Earth, it was time to head back down. Our oxygen was running low, we were exhausted, and we still had a dangerous descent ahead of us. Being careless when you are climbing down is when most accidents occur. I was determined that this would not be my last adventure, but the first of many to come.

BEAR SAYS

Focus is essential on any mission. Achieving the summit is only half the adventure. Getting back in one piece is the key goal!

K2

BEAR SAYS

K2 is the second-highest mountain in the world ... and one of the deadliest. For every four climbers to reach the summit, one dies in the attempt.

The Karakoram

The Karakoram range stands north of the Himalayas, where India, Pakistan, and China meet. Four of the world's 14 peaks that exceed 26,250 feet rise here, amid a vast area of magnificent ice-hung mountains, savage rock pillars, immense glaciers, and steep gorges. It is inhospitable, arid country, sparsely inhabited by Balti and Hunza tribespeople whose small villages, surrounded by fields and orchards, cling to ledges in the deep valleys. For a long time, this region was inaccessible and politically sensitive. In the 19th century, it was of interest to czarist Russia to its north and British India to its south. The first exploration and mapping of the Karakoram was the result of competition between the two empires. They both wanted to know more about the remote region that lay between them. It is still a sensitive region today; the Indo-Pakistan Kashmir ceasefire line cuts across the southeastern corner of the range.

K2's sharp fang on the far right, 16 miles distant, as seen from the summit of Gasherbrum I. Gasherbrums IV, III, and II are on the left.

Sir Francis Younghusband (1863–1942) has been called the last great imperial adventurer. As a cavalry officer in India, a mountain explorer, and later as a soldier-diplomat and mystic, he traveled widely in the Karakoram, one of few Englishmen to do so.

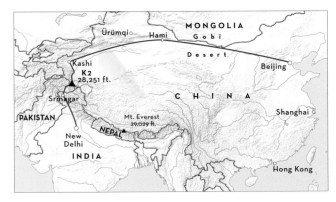

In 1887, returning to India from Peking (now Beijing), Younghusband rode across the Gobi Desert and through the unexplored Kuen-lun and Aghil ranges. He passed K2 on its northern side and crossed into India via the Muztagh Pass.

The distant Karakoram Peak 2 was seen by a British surveyor in 1856 and first approached in 1861 by Lt. Col. Godwin-Austen when he was mapping the Baltoro Glacier. He confirmed the height of K2.

Arid landscape

In 1892, Martin Conway, an art historian and alpinist, led a climbing and exploring expedition, supported by the Royal Geographical Society, into the Braldu Valley to explore the Baltoro Glacier. He named Concordia, Broad Peak, and Hidden Peak (Gasherbrum I), reached the foot of K2, and climbed the 22,598-foot Pioneer Peak.

Military mission

In 1903–04, Younghusband led a military mission to remote Lhasa. His intention was to demand a treaty of cooperation with Britain. This plan, which would have given Britain some influence in the region, was not without opposition.

The Duke of Abruzzi's 1909 expedition closely examined the south, east, and west flanks of K2. Among the group was Vittorio Sella (1859–1943), regarded as the best of the early mountain photographers. He also climbed and photographed in the Himalayas, the Caucasus, Africa, and Alaska.

Trekking to K2

The local people know the peak towering over the Baltoro Glacier as Gasherbrum, "The Shining Wall." Climbers now know it as Gasherbrum IV. G V and G VI, "Twins," are seen on the right.

Any approach to K2 is an expedition in its own right. On the usual (southern) route from Pakistan, everything must be carried by local porters. A four-wheel-drive track, frequently cut by landslides, now follows the hazardous Braldu Gorge to Askole, the last habitation. Previously, this stretch took four strenuous days on foot. Continuing up the valley and crossing the tributary Damodar River, it takes three days of hard trekking to reach the snout of the Baltoro Glacier. After four more days, this avenue of endless moraines, with few decent campsites but lined with spectacular peaks, leads to Concordia, the wide glacial T-junction from where K2 is at last visible. From here, the mountain is a mere day's march northward up the Godwin-Austen Glacier. This is the easy way—the approach to the northern side of K2, from barren Xinjiang, is even more demanding.

BEAR SAYS

The characteristic Karakoram "jola" bridges are made from plaited poplar twigs. Once common, many have now been replaced by wire-rope suspension bridges.

K2 stands on the Pakistan–Chinese border in a forest of savage peaks, surrounded by huge glaciers that drain south to the Indus River or north to high Asian deserts.

BEAR SAYS

Terraced rocky plots of barley, stands of poplar and fruit trees, goats grazing dusty pastures, and a network of irrigation channels surround the low, flat-roofed houses of Balti villages.

High altitude weather

The prevailing Karakoram summer weather comes from arid central Asia and is usually settled, until interrupted by the Indian monsoon. The monsoon can cause powerful storms, made worse on K2 by altitude and local winds. Winter snowfall is heavy; summer snowmelt makes major rivers impassable and minor streams dangerous. Travelers have been killed by rockfalls and landslides in the Braldu Gorge below Askole.

Hazardous crossing

To reach the northern side of K2, expeditions use camels. They must cross the Aghil Pass before fording the hazardous Shaksgam River. Climbers must carry all supplies the final 10 miles, which are impassable for pack animals.

Three attempts

ATTEMPTS TO REACH THE SUMMIT

1902	Oscar Eckenstein, Anglo-Austrian	NE Ridge	21,325 ft.
1909	Duke of Abruzzi, Italian	SE Ridge (Abruzzi Spur)	19,685 ft.
1938	Charles Houston, US	Abruzzi Spur	25,590 ft.

Martin Conway's expedition first reached the foot of K2 in 1892, and 10 years later, Oscar Eckenstein's team set foot on the northeast ridge. But after the Duke of Abruzzi's 1909 expedition had identified the "Abruzzi Spur" as the most feasible route, even climbing a little way up it, it was clear that K2 was too high and too difficult for climbers at that time. But experience in high-altitude mountaineering developed quickly during the 1920s. At the same time, many areas that had been blank on the Karakoram map were explored. Veteran mountaineer Eric Shipton, with a small party, reached the northern foot of K2 in 1937 and explored new ground, coming to the conclusion that any route from that side was impractical. But by 1938, climbers were ready to attempt K2 once more. Three major attempts were made before anyone succeeded.

The north face of K2 as seen from K2 glacier, Karakoram, Xinjiang, China.

1938 attempt

Charles Houston's capable 1938 team was a reconnaissance for a 1939 attempt. Bill House led the climb up a difficult rock chimney that would later be named for him. They pitched their highest camp, Camp 7, just below the Shoulder. Houston and one other team member probed a little higher before turning back, exhausted.

1939 attempt

Fritz Wiessner and Dudley Wolfe, an inept climber, pushed ahead with Sherpa Pasang Lama to Camp 8, below the Shoulder. Leaving Wolfe, they placed Camp 9 at 26,247 feet, and avoiding the Bottleneck couloir, climbed difficult rock on the left. Later, all three descended to Camp 7 for supplies, only to find, due to misunderstanding, all camps abandoned. Wiessner and Pasang Lama continued to Base Camp and sent three Sherpas up to rescue Wolfe. All four disappeared.

Master climber

Fritz Wiessner (1900-88), was born in Germany but emigrated to the United States and became a US citizen. He was an excellent rock climber with a fine record on big mountains, but he was not always an effective team leader.

Perilous climb

The most hazardous part of the Abruzzi route is the final stretch of 1,968 feet. Above the comparatively easy slopes of the Shoulder, a rock band surmounted by a band of seracs (ice cliffs) bars progress. A snow-and-ice couloir, known as the Bottleneck, leads through the rock to an exposed traverse beneath the ice cliffs.

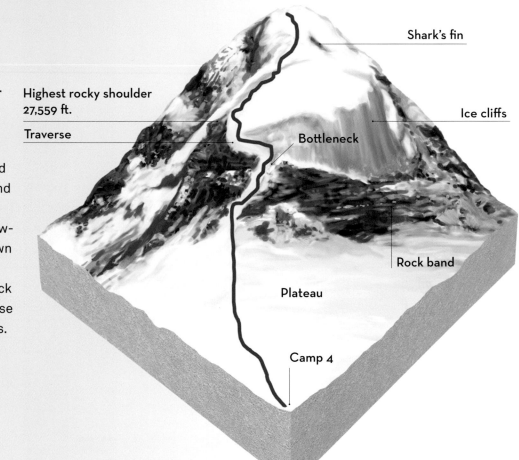

Shark's fin

Highest rocky shoulder 27,559 ft.

Traverse

Ice cliffs

Bottleneck

Rock band

Plateau

Camp 4

1953 attempt

Charles Houston chose a strong team for the 1953 attempt. All went well until a severe storm trapped all eight climbers at Camp 8. After five days, Art Gilkey became sick with thrombophlebitis—blood clots that are potentially fatal at high altitude. After eight days, a slight let up in the weather allowed the team to start descending to Camp 7, carefully lowering Gilkey on a makeshift stretcher. Climbing down across the final slope toward the camp, Robert Craig un-roped to lead the way. Then a terrible accident occurred, and the party was saved only by Peter Schoening's expertise. Gilkey, safe at first, was swept away and disappeared.

Near-fatal slip

Schoening was lowering the stretcher from his belay when one man slipped, pulled another off, cannoned into the other three, and, in a tangle of ropes, still tied to Gilkey, they all hurtled down the ice toward oblivion.

Schoening's skill

When the fall came, anticipating the shock, Schoening allowed the rope to slide a short way before locking it. It stretched and stretched, and then held. Tying off the belayed stretcher, he climbed down to help the others.

BEAR SAYS

Never underestimate the importance of experience when tackling a challenging mountain. If it weren't for Schoening's expertise, the whole party might have lost their lives.

Expert technique

Schoening belayed on a boulder embedded in the ice, arranging the ropes around his waist and ice ax so that the tension would force the ax farther into the ice.

Forbidding mountain

Mountaineering expeditions depend on careful planning, as ever-smaller camps are placed higher and higher up the mountain. Teamwork is essential, and even if only one climber reaches the summit, the expedition is considered a success. The successful 1954 expedition, and several later, used bottled oxygen. But once a mountain has been climbed without oxygen, its use is usually avoided. Sickness takes its toll, and careful acclimatization to altitude is essential.

Members of the American 1975 expedition sort ration packs at their base camp at 17,585 feet on the Savoia Glacier. As a result of tensions on the frontier, this was the first expedition permitted for 15 years, and the 10-climber team attempted the northwest ridge. The climbers reached only 21,982 feet, but they were climbing a completely unknown route.

BEAR SAYS

The lammergeier vulture (*Gypaetus barbatus*) frequents the barren landscape below the glaciers, where it searches for carrion.

Angel Peak

K2 summit
28,251 ft.

Bottleneck

Shoulder

West ridge route

Mushroom

Hockey
Stick Gully

Southwest
pillar route
"Magic Line"

Black Pyramid

American NE
ridge route

Negrotto Col

S.S.E. Spur
route

House's Chimney

South face
Polish route

Abruzzi
Spur route

De Filippi
Glacier

Slopes of Broad Peak

Godwin-Austen Glacier

Porters' loads

Sorting loads at Base Camp, each box a single porter's load (right). The skilled and professional way porters handle their loads, usually on a headband, is amazing. Good logistics are essential to the success of any expedition. Not only must hundreds of loads reach the mountain safely, but the flow of essential supplies up the mountain must be carefully organized and maintained.

Camp cooking

Base Camp (left) may be no holiday, but the conditions are comfortable, with hot food available to keep morale up. Chapattis—flat, unleavened breads—are the staple diet of porters. They are made from coarse barley flour and water, and the dough is energetically kneaded. Chapattis are traditionally cooked on a hot stone, but often now on an iron plate.

Camp porters

Two porters (right) carry supplies between camps. Most porters are local people who know the terrain well, and are well acclimatized to living at high altitude. There is a mutual respect between porters and climbers, and most expeditions would fail without the expertise and support of local porters.

Nine camps to the top

The Italian team that made the first successful ascent of K2 in 1954 used most of the eight campsites the American team had chosen in 1938 when they first felt their way up the Abruzzi Spur. Suitable tent platforms are rare on the Spur, and features such as House's Chimney and the Black Pyramid dictated the sites of Camps 4–7. Camp 9, established by the 1954 Italian team, allowed a relatively short final push to the summit. In 1979, on the third successful ascent of the route, Reinhold Messner and Michl Dacher placed their third camp close to the usual Camp 7, to climb to the summit from a fourth, very high, bivouac camp—without using oxygen.

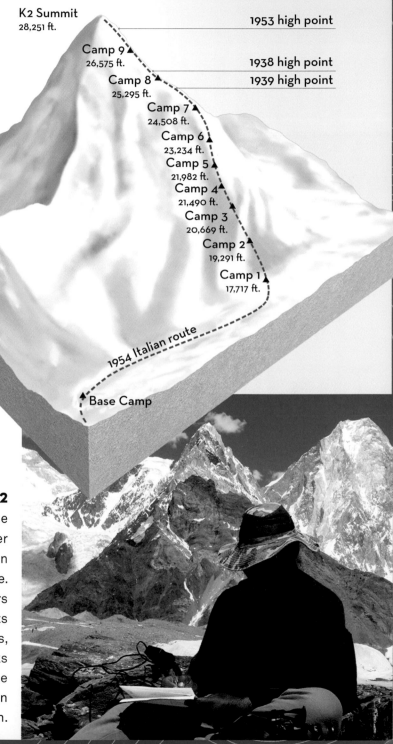

K2 Summit
28,251 ft.

1953 high point

Camp 9
26,575 ft.

1938 high point

Camp 8
25,295 ft.

1939 high point

Camp 7
24,508 ft.

Camp 6
23,234 ft.

Camp 5
21,982 ft.

Camp 4
21,490 ft.

Camp 3
20,669 ft.

Camp 2
19,291 ft.

Camp 1
17,717 ft.

1954 Italian route

Base Camp

In view of K2

Concordia is the glacial T-junction where the Godwin-Austen Glacier joins the Baltoro Glacier and K2 is first seen. Here, a climber rests in the camp at Concordia with K2 in the distance. Compared to the harsh conditions that climbers face farther up the mountain, Concordia, with its breathtaking scenery and comfortable camps, is luxury. Large expeditions employ local cooks and other camp staff on the trek in, and at Base Camp. The climbers must manage their own camps higher up the mountain.

The first ascent of K2, in 1954, was a great achievement for the Italian team. The many climbers who have reached the summit since then share the same feeling of elation.

The first ascent

The Duke of Abruzzi's 1909 expedition had given Italian climbers a special interest in K2, and in July 1954, Professor Ardito Desio mounted a large, nationally backed expedition of 11 climbers, four scientists, a doctor, and a filmmaker. They planned to use oxygen—not used previously on K2. Each oxygen set weighed 40 pounds, and consequently some 700 porters were employed for the march in. After two weeks' climbing, Camp 4 was pitched below House's Chimney. But the weather was poor, team member Mario Puchoz died from pulmonary edema, and morale sagged. Desio, himself a non-climber, sent a message to the lead team telling them that the honor of Italian mountaineering was at stake. But six weeks passed before climbers Achille Compagnoni and Lino Lacedelli established Camp 8 at 25,394 feet, just below the Shoulder. They were supported by Walter Bonatti, the youngest but most talented climber, and Pino Gallotti. All were exhausted.

The great southern flank of K2 rears some 11,483 feet over the Godwin-Austen Glacier.

Struggle to the summit

While Compagnoni and Lacedelli set up Camp 9, Bonatti and a Hunza porter, Mahdi, were bringing up more oxygen from below to deliver to them. But Camp 9 was higher than planned, night fell before they could reach it, and Bonatti and Mahdi endured a grim bivouac in the open at 26,247 feet. In the morning they retreated; Mahdi was severely frostbitten. Compagnoni and Lacedelli climbed down to collect the dumped oxygen cylinders, ascended the rock beside the Bottleneck, crossed the Traverse, and eventually reached the summit.

A climber (below) tackles the tricky snow ridge between Camps 1 and 2. The views from this spot are spectacular.

Dangerous mountain

Danger is ever-present on a big mountain, affecting even expert climbers. Falls due to carelessness are rare; the main dangers come from nature. Storms can be killers, particularly on K2, where the high camps are easily cut off. Both mind and body deteriorate swiftly at high altitude, where pulmonary edema, a life-threatening condition; phlebitis; and some other potentially fatal ailments are impossible to treat. Avalanche danger is always present, and while unstable new snow is dangerous, Karakoram ice avalanches can be unpredictable and horrific. All ice gradually moves downhill, and when a serac finally collapses it sweeps all before it. Concealed snow bridges, which are almost impossible to detect, can collapse, sending climbers falling into a deep crevasse.

Once a rope can be gotten down to a fallen climber, they should be able to climb to the surface, assuming no serious injury. This strenuous technique requires a jumar device or prusik knot, which slides up a rope but locks under tension.

Serious challenge

Many consider K2 the most beautiful, probably the most difficult, and undoubtedly the most dangerous of the world's 14 highest peaks—those above 26,250 feet. A climber has to be not only competent, but also well acclimatized to get high enough on K2 to make a summit bid. But 23,000 feet is no place to wait for better weather, and a storm at 26,250 feet is a fight for survival. Descending is particularly dangerous. Once the summit has been reached, adrenaline is exhausted, tiredness dulls the senses, and gathering dusk makes finding the route more difficult.

WOMEN AT THE SUMMIT OF K2		
1986	Wanda Rutkiewicz, Poland	Died later on Kangchenjunga
1986	Liliane Barrard, France	Killed while descending
1986	Julie Tullis, England	Died in storm on descent
1992	Chantal Mauduit, France	Died later on Dhaulagiri
1992	Alison Hargreaves, England	Died in storm on descent
2004	Edurne Pasaban, Spain	
2006	Nives Meroi, Italy	
2006	Yuka Komatsu, Japan	
2007	Eun-sun Oh, Korea	
2008	Cecilie Skog, Norway	

Storm engulfing K2 above Godwin-Austen Glacier.

At first it was said that there was a jinx on the women who had climbed K2, but high-altitude mountaineering is always a dangerous activity. Up to and including the 2008 season, a total of 302 people had reached the summit of K2, 31 of whom had been killed descending.

BEAR SAYS

Wanda Rutkiewicz was the leading female climber of her generation. She reached the summit of K2 in 1986, descending safely when 13 others died. She disappeared attempting Kangchenjunga, solo, in 1992.

Denali

Denali, Alaska,
satellite image

BEAR SAYS

As the tallest mountain in North America, Denali is one of the "Seven Summits"—the tallest mountains on each continent, a challenge for only the most courageous of mountaineers.

The Great One

Meaning "the Great One," Denali was renamed "Mount McKinley" in 1896 after William McKinley, the 25th president, and only officially returned to its original Alaskan name in 2015. Denali is a colossal, icy complex of ridges, spurs, buttresses, and hanging glaciers. It rises to twin summits, dwarfing the other peaks of the Alaska Range. Situated between the warm, damp Pacific and the cold Alaskan interior, the mountain, just 150 miles from the Arctic Circle, is a crucible of particularly evil weather. Several early attempts to climb Denali failed. One group of climbers in 1906 claimed to have reached the summit, but this was later found to have been a deception. In 1910, a party of six did reach the north summit, but it was not until 1913 that Hudson Stuck, Archdeacon of the Yukon, with three companions, claimed the south summit, 850 feet higher. The few climbers who reached the summit before 1951 followed a route on the mountain's northeast side, via the Muldrow Glacier.

BEAR SAYS

Robert Tatum, one of the first people to reach the summit of Denali, exclaimed, "The view from the top of [Denali] is like looking out the windows of Heaven!"

A female mountaineer approaches the summit of Denali; at 20,322 feet it's the highest peak in North America.

Denali, its south and north summits conspicuous, is seen here from the northeast near Polychrome Mountain on the Denali Highway.

Approaching the summit

At just above 15,748 feet, a climber slowly ascends the West Buttress crest, the regular route used by most parties. Mount Foraker, the second-highest peak in the Alaska Range, rises beyond.

Crevasse danger

Even on flat glaciers, the crevasses are deep and often hidden. Wise climbers travel roped up, so that if they do fall into a crevasse they have a good chance of climbing back to the top.

Glacier highway

Except in emergencies, aircraft are forbidden to land on glaciers in the declared wilderness area surrounding Denali, so climbers face long ski approaches up highly crevassed glacier highways. Towing their equipment on a pulk—a simple lightweight sled originating in Lapland—this climber descends the Muldrow Glacier.

Locating Denali

The culminating peak of the 400-mile Alaska Range, Denali stands at the heart of the Denali National Park, 130 miles from the state capital, Anchorage.

Highest peak in North America

Its summit standing well above others in the surrounding range, the scale of Denali is truly Himalayan, and its location, close to the Arctic Circle, accentuates the effects of high altitude—ice, blizzards, thin air, and avalanches. Dozens of challenging routes up the mountain attract the world's best mountaineers. Most celebrated is the Cassin Ridge on the south face, which was first climbed by an Italian team in 1961. They took 23 days to reach the summit, establishing a number of camps as they climbed. Strict park service regulations govern access and climbing within the national park; climbing permits must be applied for in advance.

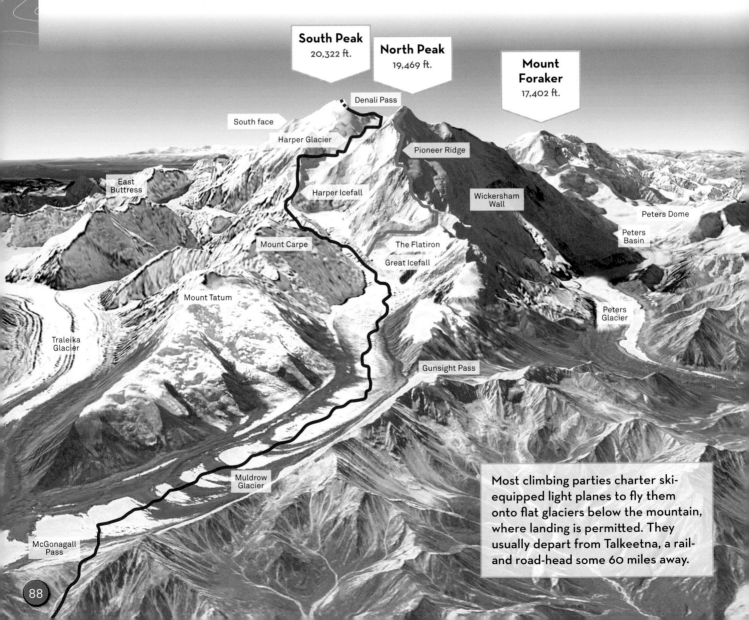

South Peak
20,322 ft.

North Peak
19,469 ft.

Mount Foraker
17,402 ft.

Denali Pass

South face

Harper Glacier

Pioneer Ridge

East Buttress

Harper Icefall

Wickersham Wall

Peters Dome

Peters Basin

Mount Carpe

The Flatiron

Great Icefall

Mount Tatum

Peters Glacier

Traleika Glacier

Gunsight Pass

Muldrow Glacier

McGonagall Pass

Most climbing parties charter ski-equipped light planes to fly them onto flat glaciers below the mountain, where landing is permitted. They usually depart from Talkeetna, a rail- and road-head some 60 miles away.

A dawn aerial view from the northeast. The first ascent party climbed Karstens Ridge to reach Harper Glacier between the south and north peaks.

Meltwater stream

The longest of the five huge glaciers radiating from Denali, the 46-mile Kahiltna Glacier extends down to 2,000 feet. At lower levels, the ice runs with water, creating meltwater streams.

The climb to the summit

A strenuous effort is needed to reach Denali's summit, yet hundreds of people climb the West Buttress route every year, many of them in guided parties. Entirely on snow, the nontechnical climb usually requires five camps. But the climb to the summit and back to Base Camp is not without danger, particularly from bad weather. The schedule for a typical guided party is 20 days. Experienced, acclimatized mountaineers could complete the climb in 10 days. The adjacent West Rib, more direct and technical, is popular with competent climbers. The south face routes and the longer ridges are for serious and committed expeditions.

The Matterhorn

BEAR SAYS

The four faces of the Matterhorn face the four cardinal directions: north, south, east, and west.

The Matterhorn, seen in early summer from the Riffelberg, a viewpoint easily reached from Zermatt. The east and north faces are to the left and right, respectively.

A rocky peak

The Matterhorn, or *Monte Cervino* in Italian, is the epitome of mountain form, carved over the eons by fierce glacial erosion from all sides. Mountains of similar shape, formed in the same way, are known as Matterhorn Peaks. The Matterhorn's name and distinctive shape are familiar everywhere. At 14,692 feet, it is only the 14th highest mountain in the European Alps, but as it stands aloof and almost completely isolated, it captures the imagination of all who see it; it has long been a popular subject for photographers.

Long, narrow valleys approach the mountain's foot from the north and south, cradling at their heads the villages of Zermatt and Breuil-Cervinia, both prime ski resorts. Since Roman times, the two valleys have been connected by the Theodule Pass, elevation 10,827 feet. It is a straightforward summer hike for those accustomed to glacier crossing, and with the proximity of ski lifts in winter, it is a route frequently used by recreational skiers visiting the neighboring resort over the frontier.

The Matterhorn is one of the knot of high, free-standing mountains at the eastern extremity of the Pennine Alps, the chain of mountains that forms part of the Swiss–Italian border.

Heavy weather

Mountain weather is always fickle. The Pennine Alps, a major European watershed dividing warm Italy and the Mediterranean from the tangled mountains and glaciers of Switzerland, are no exception. A clash of airstreams—warm or cold, humid or dry—occurs constantly. Astride that watershed, the isolated tooth of the Matterhorn attracts frequent thunderstorms that play around its summit while Zermatt, in the valley below, is bathed in sunshine. The lightning is dangerous and is often heralded by a strange humming sound that comes from ice axes and other metal equipment. If this happens, it is a good idea to temporarily dump anything metallic and take shelter below a ridge or a projecting rock.

Edward Whymper

Edward Whymper first visited Zermatt in 1860, and became keenly interested in mountaineering. At that time, no one had climbed to the Matterhorn's summit, and Whymper made that one of his goals. He also made many other notable first ascents throughout the Western Alps. After 1865, he went exploring and climbing elsewhere, making first ascents in Greenland, the Canadian Rockies, and the Andes. He died in 1911.

WHYMPER'S ATTEMPTS ON THE MATTERHORN

DATE	HEIGHT REACHED	ROUTE
Aug 29–30, 1861	12,651 ft.	Italian Ridge
Jul 7–8, 1862	12,001 ft.	Italian Ridge
Jul 9–10, 1862	12,992 ft.	Italian Ridge
Jul 18–19, 1862	13,399 ft.	Italian Ridge
Jul 23–24, 1862	13,149 ft.	Italian Ridge
Jul 25–26, 1862	13,461 ft.	Italian Ridge
Aug 10–11, 1863	13,281 ft.	Italian Ridge
Jun 21, 1865	11,201 ft.	East face

Dangerous conditions

In a bad storm, even a straightforward climb can be a fight for survival. This picture (right) shows a snowstorm on the Matterhorn's south peak. Storms like this can happen very suddenly, and the conditions can become deadly.

Whymper illustrates a fall he took while descending from the Tête du Lion after his solo attempt on July 19, 1862. Luckily, he was not badly injured.

Lanterns illuminate the original route taken by Whymper's team, to commemorate the 50th anniversary of his successful climb.

Its dramatic summit cone alight with the rays of a rising sun, the Matterhorn dominates its landscape. The mountain's steep rock ridges are an irresistible challenge for climbers.

The summit

By 1865, the Matterhorn was the last of the great peaks that had still not been climbed. Most persistent of the English amateurs and local Italian guides, who for several years had been competing to make the first ascent, were Englishman Edward Whymper and Jean-Antoine Carrel from Breuil-Cervina. Eleven attempts were made on the Italian Ridge, which appeared to be the easiest route, before the summit was finally reached via the Hornli Ridge. Whymper teamed up with Rev. Charles Hudson, Douglas Hadow, Lord Francis Douglas, and their respective guides, and led them to the summit on July 14, 1865. A terrible accident on the descent became the most analyzed and controversial in mountaineering history. Accusations were made that a vital rope had been cut, but in fact it was a worn-out spare used by mistake.

Fatal descent

The fatal accident occurred on the exposed ground above the Shoulder, a succession of small ledges separated by short steps and dusted with snow. Descending carefully, Croz led with Hadow next, then Hudson and Douglas. The two other guides, both named Taugwalder, and Whymper followed. All were roped together, but modern belays were unknown. It seems that Croz was assisting Hadow when the latter slipped, knocking Croz from his footing. The tight rope jerked Hudson and then Douglas from their holds. Whymper and the Taugwalders braced themselves to hold the fall, but the rope snapped behind Douglas. The four men plunged down the north face.

A commemorative plaque near the church of Zermatt shows the names of the 7-member rope team, British climbers Edward Whymper, Reverend Charles Hudson, Francis Douglas, Douglas Robert Hadow, and Swiss climbers Peter Taugwalder (father) and Peter Taugwalder (son) and French climber Michel Croz, who reached the Matterhorn peak for the first time. Hudson, Hadow, Douglas, and Croz, one of the finest Chamonix guides of the age, lost their lives during the descent.

Erstbesteigung Matterhorn
über Hörnligrat
13. / 14. Juli 1865

Edward Whymper
Reverend Charles Hudson
Lord Francis Douglas
Douglas Robert Hadow
Taugwalder Peter, Vater
Taugwalder Peter, Sohn
Michel Auguste Croz

Many routes to the top

The ascent of the Matterhorn, last of the great peaks to be climbed, ended the "Golden Age of Alpinism" (1854–1865), and climbers started to explore other, more difficult, routes to the summit. This so-called "Silver Age" continued into the 1900s. Almost invariably, the early mountaineers had climbed with guides, originally local peasants who understood the terrain. The best of these soon became a corps of elite, skilled mountaineers who developed a proud tradition of comradeship and teamwork with their employers. But this relationship was already disappearing by the beginning of the 20th century as guideless climbing became the norm, and guides became paid leaders rather than respected partners. Today, hundreds of fit but inexperienced climbers are guided up the Matterhorn's many routes every season.

Early morning light on several of the Matterhorn's neighbors; the view southward from the Zinalrothorn. The Matterhorn stands proudly on the left.

BEAR SAYS

Alpine guides, like Edward Whymper's guide, Jean-Antoine Carrel, need to be strong, experienced, and skillful.

Alpine guides

Most Alpine centers have their own licensed and qualified guides; in Alpine countries many of the best amateurs take the international guides exams. There are also fully qualified and often expert Alpine guides from elsewhere, particularly Britain. Today, most guides supplement their income by working as ski instructors or ski-tour leaders in winter.

Novice climbers who are fit but unskilled in mountaineering benefit from the experience of a professional guide. But even a well-planned climb carried out by seasoned climbers can include accidents. Avalanche dogs are skilled at finding people who have been buried beneath the snow.

Women climbers

Almost from the start, there were several women making difficult Alpine ascents. In 1871, Lucy Walker was the first woman to climb the Matterhorn; Meta Brevoort reached the summit a few days later. They were just two of several competent women climbers of the late 19th century. Although aware of some disapproval among non-climbers, these women discarded their skirts on leaving the valley, revealing sensible breeches beneath.

Dorothy Pilley
A fine alpinist, Dorothy Pilley (center) made the first ascent of the daunting north ridge of the Dent Blanche in 1928.

Annie Peck
American Annie Peck climbed widely in the Alps and the Andes. She helped found the American Alpine Club in 1902.

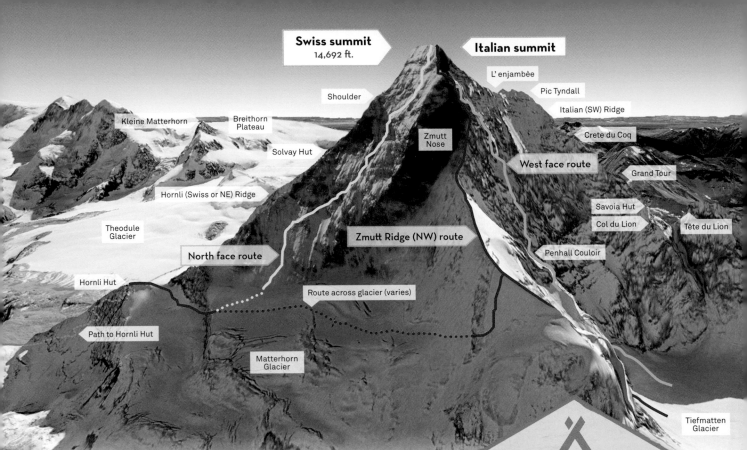

Swiss summit 14,692 ft.

Italian summit

L' enjambêe

Pic Tyndall

Shoulder

Italian (SW) Ridge

Kleine Matterhorn

Breithorn Plateau

Crete du Coq

Zmutt Nose

Solvay Hut

West face route

Grand Tour

Hornli (Swiss or NE) Ridge

Savoia Hut

Col du Lion

Tête du Lion

Theodule Glacier

Zmutt Ridge (NW) route

North face route

Penhall Couloir

Hornli Hut

Route across glacier (varies)

Path to Hornli Hut

Matterhorn Glacier

Tiefmatten Glacier

Many ridges and faces

Once the summit had been reached via the Hornli and Italian ridges, there were still two ridges and four faces for climbers to attempt. The challenging Zmutt Ridge and the tottering west face were both climbed successfully in 1879. The east face and the complex south face are hazardous climbs because of crumbling rock and dangerous stone falls. They were both climbed by Italian teams in the early 1930s, but are rarely climbed now. Three steep towers mark the Furggen Ridge. The final overhangs on this route were not directly climbed until 1941.

BEAR SAYS

The marmot's shrill warning whistle is familiar to all who frequent the Alps. Marmots live in burrows below the snow line.

Choosing a route

The route most often climbed on the Matterhorn is the Hornli Ridge route; in summer, mountain guides lead many people to the summit via this route. But the bleak north face continues to be a challenge to be tackled by only the most experienced of climbers.

The classic Zmutt, or northwest ridge, was pioneered by Albert Mummery with Alexander Burgener in 1879. It is considered the finest climb on the Matterhorn. The west face, made extremely dangerous by rockfall, is rarely climbed.

Situated at the head of the long Matter Valley, and once a simple mountain village, Zermatt (left) is today a world-class, luxury mountain resort, center of a magnificent ski area and accessible only by railway.

Rock falls

The Matterhorn, like every other mountain, is gradually disintegrating, as thousands of tons of rock fall every year. In 2003, massive rock avalanches stranded 90 climbers on the Hornli Ridge. They had to be evacuated by helicopter.

The regular climb up the Matterhorn starts at the Hornli Hut at 10,696 feet, reached after a stiff hike. Built in 1880, it now includes a simple hotel. There are some 2,000 climbers' huts throughout the Alps.

Climbers are seen on the western (Italian) summit of the Matterhorn. The Swiss summit, just 262 feet distant along the narrow crest, is 3 feet higher.

More challenges

The first ascent of any new route, and especially of any new mountain, attracts praise and congratulations. The achievement is often a source of competition, too. A first ascent is always the most difficult, but once a route is repeated and details of the climb are described in a guidebook, adventurous climbers look for more challenging routes. This is what happened on the Matterhorn. The more difficult Italian Ridge was climbed three days after Whymper's ascent of the Hornli Ridge, then in 1879 came the more serious Zmutt Ridge climb. The awkward Furggen Ridge was not climbed successfully until 1911. The daunting north face, a very serious commitment, awaited a new generation of climbers armed with new techniques. Several attempts were repulsed until Franz and Toni Schmid, brothers who were unknown to other alpinists, arrived in Zermatt from Munich on their bicycles.

In 1931, on their first visit to the western Alps, Franz and Toni Schmid, brothers from Munich, climbed the intimidating Matterhorn north face with only one bivouac. The climb was repeated only twice in 15 years.

The Alpine Club

The original Alpine Club was founded in 1857, with premises in London. Club members must be experienced mountaineers, and the membership includes leading climbers from many nations. National Alpine Clubs were also founded in the 19th century—Austrian in 1862, Swiss and Italian in 1863, French in 1874. These clubs own most of the Alpine huts, and members enjoy reciprocal rights.

The Matterhorn's north face

In the northern hemisphere, the typical north face is shadowed, steep, and icy—all features that are seen in the Alps. The north faces were the final climbing routes to be explored, and by the mid-1920s, keen climbers were attempting them. The Matterhorn's north face, with no obvious weakness, its rocky scales permanently iced, was a major prize. It defeated several attempts.

Gear and techniques

Primitive at first, climbing equipment, clothing, and techniques improved only gradually. Hemp ropes were useful for safety, but they did not guarantee survival in a fall. On steep ice, steps had to be cut. Major developments occurred in the eastern Alps in the early 1900s, where difficult rock climbs produced innovative rope techniques and inspired new gear such as pitons and carabiners. These were soon used on the big mountains, too. Nylon ropes, first seen in the late 1940s, revolutionized climbing. Modern ice tools originated in Scotland in the 1960s and 1970s.

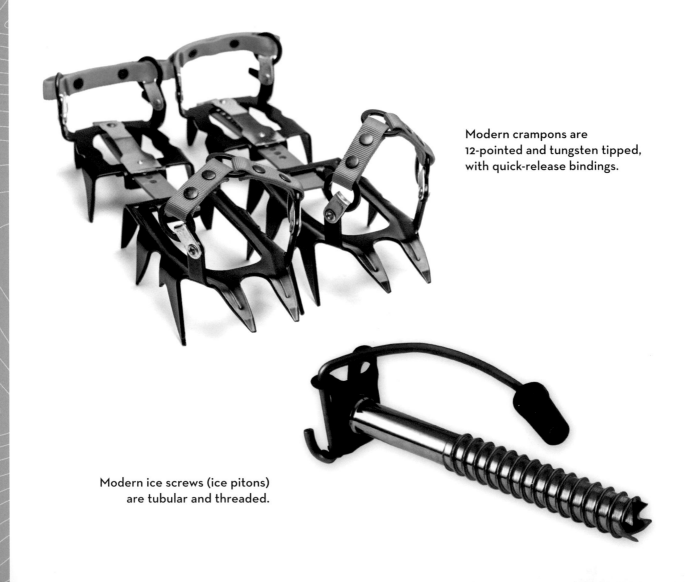

Modern crampons are 12-pointed and tungsten tipped, with quick-release bindings.

Modern ice screws (ice pitons) are tubular and threaded.

Specialist ice tools —hammer and adze, designed for climbing vertical frozen waterfalls.

Carabiners—lightweight snap links of high-tech alloy with twist-lock gates.

Modern ropes—man-made fiber, sheathed "kernmantle" construction.

Glossary

Abseil: Literally "down-rope" in German, a rapid method of descent using the rope to slide down, but controlling the slide by friction.

Altitude sickness: Illness suffered at altitudes where the air is thin. It can range from headaches at lower altitudes to potentially fatal conditions.

Belay: The dynamic rope-handling technique used by climbers to safeguard themselves and their companions from a fall. Also the rock spike or piton used to attach the rope.

Bivouac: A temporary overnight camp in the open.

Carabiner: An oval or D-shaped snap-link usually made from lightweight alloy, which opens with a sprung gate.

Chimney: A vertical fissure, usually in rock, and at least wide enough to admit the body.

Couloir: A gully on a mountainside, usually snow or ice filled. May be a steep chute, and therefore a natural channel for falling rocks and avalanches.

Crevasse: A crack, which may be deep, in the surface of a glacier or ice field. When bridged with snow, a crevasse is difficult to detect.

Cwm: The universally adopted Welsh name for a deep valley head, on a hanging valley of glacial origin. Also "cirque."

Hanging ice field: A miniature glacier apparently stuck on to the face of a mountain, likely to be less steep than the surrounding cliffs and walls.

Icefall: A cataract of ice, always moving, formed when a glacier flows over a rock step or steep ground, or is constricted between mountain walls.

Jumar: A small metal device which, when clipped to a rope, will slide up it but not down.

Moraine: Rock debris, rubble, and boulders brought down by a glacier, which may form long ridges or high mounds lying on, beside, or below the glacier. Often unstable.

Piton: A small metal spike, variously shaped, that can be hammered into a crack in the rock. Ice pitons, longer and tubular, are screwed into ice.

Prusik knot: A simple friction hitch. It can be freely pushed up when slack, but locks under tension. Used for climbing a hanging rope.

Pulmonary edema: An excessive accumulation of fluid in the lungs caused by altitude. Fatal at high altitude, treatable by immediate descent.

Ski mountaineer: A mountaineer who climbs mountains on specially fitted skis. Even steep snow slopes can be ascended swiftly and easily.

Scree: Loose rock fragments ranging in size from pebbles to small boulders. Usually found on the slopes below cliffs or on ledges.

Terrestrial: On dry land.

Traverse: Moving sideways as opposed to upward or downward.

Watershed: The dividing line, usually following a ridge or high ground, between the catchments of two river systems.

Picture Credits

Index